Flawed

Introduction

Flawed But Still Chosen By God is a devotional journey for every believer who has ever questioned their worth,
doubted their calling, or felt too broken to be used by God. This book is a reminder that God doesn't require perfection-He desires your surrender.
He sees beyond your mistakes and insecurities and chooses you anyway.

Each of the 72 chapters in this book represents a step in understanding your identity in Christ. You'll walk through seasons of doubt, healing, purpose, and victory, discovering that your flaws don't disqualify you-they position you for grace.

This book is meant to be more than just read-it's meant to be experienced. Take time with each chapter. Reflect on the scriptures.
Write down your thoughts. Pray through the struggles. Let this be a sacred space where God reminds you that He has chosen you, still.

You are not overlooked. You are not forgotten. You are flawed, yes-but you are chosen.

- Shanequa Robinson

Table of Contents

Chapter 1: Called But Insecure

Chapter 2: Broken but Chosen

Chapter 3: Recognizing the Call - Lesson 3

Chapter 4: Recognizing the Call - Lesson 4

Chapter 5: Recognizing the Call - Lesson 5

Chapter 6: Recognizing the Call - Lesson 6

Chapter 7: Recognizing the Call - Lesson 7

Chapter 8: Recognizing the Call - Lesson 8

Chapter 9: Recognizing the Call - Lesson 9

Chapter 10: Recognizing the Call - Lesson 10

Chapter 11: Recognizing the Call - Lesson 11

Chapter 12: Recognizing the Call - Lesson 12

Chapter 13: Recognizing the Call - Lesson 13

Chapter 14: Recognizing the Call - Lesson 14

Chapter 15: Facing the Flaws - Lesson 15

Chapter 16: Facing the Flaws - Lesson 16

Chapter 17: Facing the Flaws - Lesson 17

Chapter 18: Facing the Flaws - Lesson 18

Chapter 19: Facing the Flaws - Lesson 19

Chapter 20: Facing the Flaws - Lesson 20

Chapter 21: Facing the Flaws - Lesson 21

Chapter 22: Facing the Flaws - Lesson 22

Chapter 23: Facing the Flaws - Lesson 23

Chapter 24: Facing the Flaws - Lesson 24

Chapter 25: Facing the Flaws - Lesson 25

Chapter 26: Facing the Flaws - Lesson 26

Chapter 27: Wrestling with Doubt - Lesson 27

Chapter 28: Wrestling with Doubt - Lesson 28

Chapter 29: Wrestling with Doubt - Lesson 29

Chapter 30: Wrestling with Doubt - Lesson 30

Chapter 31: Wrestling with Doubt - Lesson 31

Chapter 32: Wrestling with Doubt - Lesson 32

Chapter 33: Wrestling with Doubt - Lesson 33

Chapter 34: Wrestling with Doubt - Lesson 34

Chapter 35: Wrestling with Doubt - Lesson 35

Chapter 36: Wrestling with Doubt - Lesson 36

Chapter 37: Wrestling with Doubt - Lesson 37

Chapter 38: Wrestling with Doubt - Lesson 38

Chapter 39: God's Grace & Redemption - Lesson 39

Chapter 40: God's Grace & Redemption - Lesson 40

Chapter 41: God's Grace & Redemption - Lesson 41

Chapter 42: God's Grace & Redemption - Lesson 42

Chapter 43: God's Grace & Redemption - Lesson 43

Chapter 44: God's Grace & Redemption - Lesson 44

Chapter 45: God's Grace & Redemption - Lesson 45

Chapter 46: God's Grace & Redemption - Lesson 46

Chapter 47: God's Grace & Redemption - Lesson 47

Chapter 48: God's Grace & Redemption - Lesson 48

Chapter 49: God's Grace & Redemption - Lesson 49

Chapter 50: God's Grace & Redemption - Lesson 50

Chapter 51: Walking in Purpose - Lesson 51

Chapter 52: Walking in Purpose - Lesson 52

Chapter 53: Walking in Purpose - Lesson 53

Chapter 54: Walking in Purpose - Lesson 54

Chapter 55: Walking in Purpose - Lesson 55

Chapter 56: Walking in Purpose - Lesson 56

Chapter 57: Walking in Purpose - Lesson 57

Chapter 58: Walking in Purpose - Lesson 58

Chapter 59: Walking in Purpose - Lesson 59

Chapter 60: Walking in Purpose - Lesson 60

Chapter 61: Walking in Purpose - Lesson 61

Chapter 62: Walking in Purpose - Lesson 62

Chapter 63: Living Chosen Daily - Lesson 63

Chapter 64: Living Chosen Daily - Lesson 64

Chapter 65: Living Chosen Daily - Lesson 65

Chapter 66: Living Chosen Daily - Lesson 66

Chapter 67: Living Chosen Daily - Lesson 67

Chapter 68: Living Chosen Daily - Lesson 68

Chapter 69: Living Chosen Daily - Lesson 69

Chapter 70: Living Chosen Daily - Lesson 70

Chapter 71: Living Chosen Daily - Lesson 71

Chapter 72: Living Chosen Daily - Lesson 72

Chapter 1: Called But Insecure

Scripture: Jeremiah 1:5 - This verse supports the message of Chapter 3.

Like Moses, we often question God's call on our lives because of our insecurities. We look at our past, our weaknesses, and our perceived inadequacies. But God doesn't call the qualified-He qualifies the called. Your insecurity is not a disqualifier. It's an opportunity for God to show Himself strong through you.

Journal Prompt: What insecurities are keeping you from stepping fully into your calling?

Quote: "God isn't looking for perfection-He's looking for obedience."

Prayer: Lord, remind me that You are with me even when I feel unworthy. Strengthen my faith to follow Your call.

Chapter 2: Broken but Chosen

Scripture: Romans 11:29 - This verse supports the message of Chapter 4.

Being broken doesn't make you unusable-it makes you real. God draws near to the brokenhearted. He doesn't require wholeness before He calls you. In fact, He often uses the very areas of your life that feel shattered to reflect His glory. Your brokenness is not a barrier; it's a testimony in the making.

Journal Prompt: What broken areas of your life have you been hiding from God? How might He want to use them?

Quote: "Your broken pieces are still in God's hands-and He never wastes a piece."

Prayer: God, take my brokenness and use it for Your glory. Remind me that I am still chosen.

Chapter 3: Recognizing the Call - Lesson 3

Scripture: 2 Timothy 1:9 - This verse supports the message of Chapter 5.

Chapter 3 explores the theme of 'Recognizing the Call'. In this chapter, we reflect on how God's presence, grace, and calling are evident in our lives despite our imperfections. This devotional draws from scripture to provide comfort, guidance, and inspiration as you grow in faith.

Journal Prompt: What truth stood out to you in Chapter 3? How can you live this out today?

Quote: "You are still chosen, even in your recognizing the call season."

Prayer: Lord, help me embrace Your purpose for me, especially in this area of recognizing the call.

Chapter 4: Recognizing the Call - Lesson 4

Scripture: Exodus 3:11 - This verse supports the message of Chapter 6.

Chapter 4 explores the theme of 'Recognizing the Call'. In this chapter, we reflect on how God's presence, grace, and calling are evident in our lives despite our imperfections. This devotional draws from scripture to provide comfort, guidance, and inspiration as you grow in faith.

Journal Prompt: What truth stood out to you in Chapter 4? How can you live this out today?

Quote: "You are still chosen, even in your recognizing the call season."

Prayer: Lord, help me embrace Your purpose for me, especially in this area of recognizing the call.

Chapter 5: Recognizing the Call - Lesson 5

Scripture: Isaiah 6:8 - This verse supports the message of Chapter 7.

Chapter 5 explores the theme of 'Recognizing the Call'. In this chapter, we reflect on how God's presence, grace, and calling are evident in our lives despite our imperfections. This devotional draws from scripture to provide comfort, guidance, and inspiration as you grow in faith.

Journal Prompt: What truth stood out to you in Chapter 5? How can you live this out today?

Quote: "You are still chosen, even in your recognizing the call season."

Prayer: Lord, help me embrace Your purpose for me, especially in this area of recognizing the call.

Chapter 6: Recognizing the Call - Lesson 6

Scripture: 1 Corinthians 1:26-27 - This verse supports the message of Chapter 8.

Chapter 6 explores the theme of 'Recognizing the Call'. In this chapter, we reflect on how God's presence, grace, and calling are evident in our lives despite our imperfections. This devotional draws from scripture to provide comfort, guidance, and inspiration as you grow in faith.

Journal Prompt: What truth stood out to you in Chapter 6? How can you live this out today?

Quote: "You are still chosen, even in your recognizing the call season."

Prayer: Lord, help me embrace Your purpose for me, especially in this area of recognizing the call.

Chapter 7: Recognizing the Call - Lesson 7

Scripture: John 15:16 - This verse supports the message of Chapter 9.

Chapter 7 explores the theme of 'Recognizing the Call'. In this chapter, we reflect on how God's presence, grace, and calling are evident in our lives despite our imperfections. This devotional draws from scripture to provide comfort, guidance, and inspiration as you grow in faith.

Journal Prompt: What truth stood out to you in Chapter 7? How can you live this out today?

Quote: "You are still chosen, even in your recognizing the call season."

Prayer: Lord, help me embrace Your purpose for me, especially in this area of recognizing the call.

Chapter 8: Recognizing the Call - Lesson 8

Scripture: Acts 9:15 - This verse supports the message of Chapter 10.

Chapter 8 explores the theme of 'Recognizing the Call'. In this chapter, we reflect on how God's presence, grace, and calling are evident in our lives despite our imperfections. This devotional draws from scripture to provide comfort, guidance, and inspiration as you grow in faith.

Journal Prompt: What truth stood out to you in Chapter 8? How can you live this out today?

Quote: "You are still chosen, even in your recognizing the call season."

Prayer: Lord, help me embrace Your purpose for me, especially in this area of recognizing the call.

Chapter 9: Recognizing the Call - Lesson 9

Scripture: Ephesians 2:10 - This verse supports the message of Chapter 11.

Chapter 9 explores the theme of 'Recognizing the Call'. In this chapter, we reflect on how God's presence, grace, and calling are evident in our lives despite our imperfections. This devotional draws from scripture to provide comfort, guidance, and inspiration as you grow in faith.

Journal Prompt: What truth stood out to you in Chapter 9? How can you live this out today?

Quote: "You are still chosen, even in your recognizing the call season."

Prayer: Lord, help me embrace Your purpose for me, especially in this area of recognizing the call.

Chapter 10: Recognizing the Call - Lesson 10

Scripture: Psalm 139:13-14 - This verse supports the message of Chapter 12.

Chapter 10 explores the theme of 'Recognizing the Call'. In this chapter, we reflect on how God's presence, grace, and calling are evident in our lives despite our imperfections. This devotional draws from scripture to provide comfort, guidance, and inspiration as you grow in faith.

Journal Prompt: What truth stood out to you in Chapter 10? How can you live this out today?

Quote: "You are still chosen, even in your recognizing the call season."

Prayer: Lord, help me embrace Your purpose for me, especially in this area of recognizing the call.

Chapter 11: Recognizing the Call - Lesson 11

Scripture: Galatians 1:15 - This verse supports the message of Chapter 13.

Chapter 11 explores the theme of 'Recognizing the Call'. In this chapter, we reflect on how God's presence, grace, and calling are evident in our lives despite our imperfections. This devotional draws from scripture to provide comfort, guidance, and inspiration as you grow in faith.

Journal Prompt: What truth stood out to you in Chapter 11? How can you live this out today?

Quote: "You are still chosen, even in your recognizing the call season."

Prayer: Lord, help me embrace Your purpose for me, especially in this area of recognizing the call.

Chapter 12: Recognizing the Call - Lesson 12

Scripture: Romans 8:28 - This verse supports the message of Chapter 14.

Chapter 12 explores the theme of 'Recognizing the Call'. In this chapter, we reflect on how God's presence, grace, and calling are evident in our lives despite our imperfections. This devotional draws from scripture to provide comfort, guidance, and inspiration as you grow in faith.

Journal Prompt: What truth stood out to you in Chapter 12? How can you live this out today?

Quote: "You are still chosen, even in your recognizing the call season."

Prayer: Lord, help me embrace Your purpose for me, especially in this area of recognizing the call.

Chapter 13: Recognizing the Call - Lesson 13

Scripture: Romans 3:23 - This verse supports the message of Chapter 15.

Chapter 13 explores the theme of 'Recognizing the Call'. In this chapter, we reflect on how God's presence, grace, and calling are evident in our lives despite our imperfections. This devotional draws from scripture to provide comfort, guidance, and inspiration as you grow in faith.

Journal Prompt: What truth stood out to you in Chapter 13? How can you live this out today?

Quote: "You are still chosen, even in your recognizing the call season."

Prayer: Lord, help me embrace Your purpose for me, especially in this area of recognizing the call.

Chapter 14: Recognizing the Call - Lesson 14

Scripture: 2 Corinthians 12:9 - This verse supports the message of Chapter 16.

Chapter 14 explores the theme of 'Recognizing the Call'. In this chapter, we reflect on how God's presence, grace, and calling are evident in our lives despite our imperfections. This devotional draws from scripture to provide comfort, guidance, and inspiration as you grow in faith.

Journal Prompt: What truth stood out to you in Chapter 14? How can you live this out today?

Quote: "You are still chosen, even in your recognizing the call season."

Prayer: Lord, help me embrace Your purpose for me, especially in this area of recognizing the call.

Chapter 15: Facing the Flaws - Lesson 15

Scripture: James 5:16 - This verse supports the message of Chapter 17.

Chapter 15 explores the theme of 'Facing the Flaws'. In this chapter, we reflect on how God's presence, grace, and calling are evident in our lives despite our imperfections. This devotional draws from scripture to provide comfort, guidance, and inspiration as you grow in faith.

Journal Prompt: What truth stood out to you in Chapter 15? How can you live this out today?

Quote: "You are still chosen, even in your facing the flaws season."

Prayer: Lord, help me embrace Your purpose for me, especially in this area of facing the flaws.

Chapter 16: Facing the Flaws - Lesson 16

Scripture: Psalm 51:17 - This verse supports the message of Chapter 18.

Chapter 16 explores the theme of 'Facing the Flaws'. In this chapter, we reflect on how God's presence, grace, and calling are evident in our lives despite our imperfections. This devotional draws from scripture to provide comfort, guidance, and inspiration as you grow in faith.

Journal Prompt: What truth stood out to you in Chapter 16? How can you live this out today?

Quote: "You are still chosen, even in your facing the flaws season."

Prayer: Lord, help me embrace Your purpose for me, especially in this area of facing the flaws.

Chapter 17: Facing the Flaws - Lesson 17

Scripture: 1 John 1:9 - This verse supports the message of Chapter 19.

Chapter 17 explores the theme of 'Facing the Flaws'. In this chapter, we reflect on how God's presence, grace, and calling are evident in our lives despite our imperfections. This devotional draws from scripture to provide comfort, guidance, and inspiration as you grow in faith.

Journal Prompt: What truth stood out to you in Chapter 17? How can you live this out today?

Quote: "You are still chosen, even in your facing the flaws season."

Prayer: Lord, help me embrace Your purpose for me, especially in this area of facing the flaws.

Chapter 18: Facing the Flaws - Lesson 18

Scripture: Hebrews 4:15 - This verse supports the message of Chapter 20.

Chapter 18 explores the theme of 'Facing the Flaws'. In this chapter, we reflect on how God's presence, grace, and calling are evident in our lives despite our imperfections. This devotional draws from scripture to provide comfort, guidance, and inspiration as you grow in faith.

Journal Prompt: What truth stood out to you in Chapter 18? How can you live this out today?

Quote: "You are still chosen, even in your facing the flaws season."

Prayer: Lord, help me embrace Your purpose for me, especially in this area of facing the flaws.

Chapter 19: Facing the Flaws - Lesson 19

Scripture: Isaiah 64:6 - This verse supports the message of Chapter 21.

Chapter 19 explores the theme of 'Facing the Flaws'. In this chapter, we reflect on how God's presence, grace, and calling are evident in our lives despite our imperfections. This devotional draws from scripture to provide comfort, guidance, and inspiration as you grow in faith.

Journal Prompt: What truth stood out to you in Chapter 19? How can you live this out today?

Quote: "You are still chosen, even in your facing the flaws season."

Prayer: Lord, help me embrace Your purpose for me, especially in this area of facing the flaws.

Chapter 20: Facing the Flaws - Lesson 20

Scripture: Proverbs 28:13 - This verse supports the message of Chapter 22.

Chapter 20 explores the theme of 'Facing the Flaws'. In this chapter, we reflect on how God's presence, grace, and calling are evident in our lives despite our imperfections. This devotional draws from scripture to provide comfort, guidance, and inspiration as you grow in faith.

Journal Prompt: What truth stood out to you in Chapter 20? How can you live this out today?

Quote: "You are still chosen, even in your facing the flaws season."

Prayer: Lord, help me embrace Your purpose for me, especially in this area of facing the flaws.

Chapter 21: Facing the Flaws - Lesson 21

Scripture: Luke 7:47 - This verse supports the message of Chapter 23.

Chapter 21 explores the theme of 'Facing the Flaws'. In this chapter, we reflect on how God's presence, grace, and calling are evident in our lives despite our imperfections. This devotional draws from scripture to provide comfort, guidance, and inspiration as you grow in faith.

Journal Prompt: What truth stood out to you in Chapter 21? How can you live this out today?

Quote: "You are still chosen, even in your facing the flaws season."

Prayer: Lord, help me embrace Your purpose for me, especially in this area of facing the flaws.

Chapter 22: Facing the Flaws - Lesson 22

Scripture: Mark 2:17 - This verse supports the message of Chapter 24.

Chapter 22 explores the theme of 'Facing the Flaws'. In this chapter, we reflect on how God's presence, grace, and calling are evident in our lives despite our imperfections. This devotional draws from scripture to provide comfort, guidance, and inspiration as you grow in faith.

Journal Prompt: What truth stood out to you in Chapter 22? How can you live this out today?

Quote: "You are still chosen, even in your facing the flaws season."

Prayer: Lord, help me embrace Your purpose for me, especially in this area of facing the flaws.

Chapter 23: Facing the Flaws - Lesson 23

Scripture: Romans 5:8 - This verse supports the message of Chapter 25.

Chapter 23 explores the theme of 'Facing the Flaws'. In this chapter, we reflect on how God's presence, grace, and calling are evident in our lives despite our imperfections. This devotional draws from scripture to provide comfort, guidance, and inspiration as you grow in faith.

Journal Prompt: What truth stood out to you in Chapter 23? How can you live this out today?

Quote: "You are still chosen, even in your facing the flaws season."

Prayer: Lord, help me embrace Your purpose for me, especially in this area of facing the flaws.

Chapter 24: Facing the Flaws - Lesson 24

Scripture: Micah 7:8 - This verse supports the message of Chapter 26.

Chapter 24 explores the theme of 'Facing the Flaws'. In this chapter, we reflect on how God's presence, grace, and calling are evident in our lives despite our imperfections. This devotional draws from scripture to provide comfort, guidance, and inspiration as you grow in faith.

Journal Prompt: What truth stood out to you in Chapter 24? How can you live this out today?

Quote: "You are still chosen, even in your facing the flaws season."

Prayer: Lord, help me embrace Your purpose for me, especially in this area of facing the flaws.

Chapter 25: Facing the Flaws - Lesson 25

Scripture: Mark 9:24 - This verse supports the message of Chapter 27.

Chapter 25 explores the theme of 'Facing the Flaws'. In this chapter, we reflect on how God's presence, grace, and calling are evident in our lives despite our imperfections. This devotional draws from scripture to provide comfort, guidance, and inspiration as you grow in faith.

Journal Prompt: What truth stood out to you in Chapter 25? How can you live this out today?

Quote: "You are still chosen, even in your facing the flaws season."

Prayer: Lord, help me embrace Your purpose for me, especially in this area of facing the flaws.

Chapter 26: Facing the Flaws - Lesson 26

Scripture: James 1:6 - This verse supports the message of Chapter 28.

Chapter 26 explores the theme of 'Facing the Flaws'. In this chapter, we reflect on how God's presence, grace, and calling are evident in our lives despite our imperfections. This devotional draws from scripture to provide comfort, guidance, and inspiration as you grow in faith.

Journal Prompt: What truth stood out to you in Chapter 26? How can you live this out today?

Quote: "You are still chosen, even in your facing the flaws season."

Prayer: Lord, help me embrace Your purpose for me, especially in this area of facing the flaws.

Chapter 27: Wrestling with Doubt - Lesson 27

Scripture: Matthew 14:31 - This verse supports the message of Chapter 29.

Chapter 27 explores the theme of 'Wrestling with Doubt'. In this chapter, we reflect on how God's presence, grace, and calling are evident in our lives despite our imperfections. This devotional draws from scripture to provide comfort, guidance, and inspiration as you grow in faith.

Journal Prompt: What truth stood out to you in Chapter 27? How can you live this out today?

Quote: "You are still chosen, even in your wrestling with doubt season."

Prayer: Lord, help me embrace Your purpose for me, especially in this area of wrestling with doubt.

Chapter 28: Wrestling with Doubt - Lesson 28

Scripture: Hebrews 11:1 - This verse supports the message of Chapter 30.

Chapter 28 explores the theme of 'Wrestling with Doubt'. In this chapter, we reflect on how God's presence, grace, and calling are evident in our lives despite our imperfections. This devotional draws from scripture to provide comfort, guidance, and inspiration as you grow in faith.

Journal Prompt: What truth stood out to you in Chapter 28? How can you live this out today?

Quote: "You are still chosen, even in your wrestling with doubt season."

Prayer: Lord, help me embrace Your purpose for me, especially in this area of wrestling with doubt.

Chapter 29: Wrestling with Doubt - Lesson 29

Scripture: Psalm 94:19 - This verse supports the message of Chapter 31.

Chapter 29 explores the theme of 'Wrestling with Doubt'. In this chapter, we reflect on how God's presence, grace, and calling are evident in our lives despite our imperfections. This devotional draws from scripture to provide comfort, guidance, and inspiration as you grow in faith.

Journal Prompt: What truth stood out to you in Chapter 29? How can you live this out today?

Quote: "You are still chosen, even in your wrestling with doubt season."

Prayer: Lord, help me embrace Your purpose for me, especially in this area of wrestling with doubt.

Chapter 30: Wrestling with Doubt - Lesson 30

Scripture: Matthew 28:17 - This verse supports the message of Chapter 32.

Chapter 30 explores the theme of 'Wrestling with Doubt'. In this chapter, we reflect on how God's presence, grace, and calling are evident in our lives despite our imperfections. This devotional draws from scripture to provide comfort, guidance, and inspiration as you grow in faith.

Journal Prompt: What truth stood out to you in Chapter 30? How can you live this out today?

Quote: "You are still chosen, even in your wrestling with doubt season."

Prayer: Lord, help me embrace Your purpose for me, especially in this area of wrestling with doubt.

Chapter 31: Wrestling with Doubt - Lesson 31

Scripture: Isaiah 41:10 - This verse supports the message of Chapter 33.

Chapter 31 explores the theme of 'Wrestling with Doubt'. In this chapter, we reflect on how God's presence, grace, and calling are evident in our lives despite our imperfections. This devotional draws from scripture to provide comfort, guidance, and inspiration as you grow in faith.

Journal Prompt: What truth stood out to you in Chapter 31? How can you live this out today?

Quote: "You are still chosen, even in your wrestling with doubt season."

Prayer: Lord, help me embrace Your purpose for me, especially in this area of wrestling with doubt.

Chapter 32: Wrestling with Doubt - Lesson 32

Scripture: John 20:27 - This verse supports the message of Chapter 34.

Chapter 32 explores the theme of 'Wrestling with Doubt'. In this chapter, we reflect on how God's presence, grace, and calling are evident in our lives despite our imperfections. This devotional draws from scripture to provide comfort, guidance, and inspiration as you grow in faith.

Journal Prompt: What truth stood out to you in Chapter 32? How can you live this out today?

Quote: "You are still chosen, even in your wrestling with doubt season."

Prayer: Lord, help me embrace Your purpose for me, especially in this area of wrestling with doubt.

Chapter 33: Wrestling with Doubt - Lesson 33

Scripture: Jude 1:22 - This verse supports the message of Chapter 35.

Chapter 33 explores the theme of 'Wrestling with Doubt'. In this chapter, we reflect on how God's presence, grace, and calling are evident in our lives despite our imperfections. This devotional draws from scripture to provide comfort, guidance, and inspiration as you grow in faith.

Journal Prompt: What truth stood out to you in Chapter 33? How can you live this out today?

Quote: "You are still chosen, even in your wrestling with doubt season."

Prayer: Lord, help me embrace Your purpose for me, especially in this area of wrestling with doubt.

Chapter 34: Wrestling with Doubt - Lesson 34

Scripture: 2 Corinthians 5:7 - This verse supports the message of Chapter 36.

Chapter 34 explores the theme of 'Wrestling with Doubt'. In this chapter, we reflect on how God's presence, grace, and calling are evident in our lives despite our imperfections. This devotional draws from scripture to provide comfort, guidance, and inspiration as you grow in faith.

Journal Prompt: What truth stood out to you in Chapter 34? How can you live this out today?

Quote: "You are still chosen, even in your wrestling with doubt season."

Prayer: Lord, help me embrace Your purpose for me, especially in this area of wrestling with doubt.

Chapter 35: Wrestling with Doubt - Lesson 35

Scripture: Psalm 73:26 - This verse supports the message of Chapter 37.

Chapter 35 explores the theme of 'Wrestling with Doubt'. In this chapter, we reflect on how God's presence, grace, and calling are evident in our lives despite our imperfections. This devotional draws from scripture to provide comfort, guidance, and inspiration as you grow in faith.

Journal Prompt: What truth stood out to you in Chapter 35? How can you live this out today?

Quote: "You are still chosen, even in your wrestling with doubt season."

Prayer: Lord, help me embrace Your purpose for me, especially in this area of wrestling with doubt.

Chapter 36: Wrestling with Doubt - Lesson 36

Scripture: Romans 10:17 - This verse supports the message of Chapter 38.

Chapter 36 explores the theme of 'Wrestling with Doubt'. In this chapter, we reflect on how God's presence, grace, and calling are evident in our lives despite our imperfections. This devotional draws from scripture to provide comfort, guidance, and inspiration as you grow in faith.

Journal Prompt: What truth stood out to you in Chapter 36? How can you live this out today?

Quote: "You are still chosen, even in your wrestling with doubt season."

Prayer: Lord, help me embrace Your purpose for me, especially in this area of wrestling with doubt.

Chapter 37: Wrestling with Doubt - Lesson 37

Scripture: Ephesians 2:8-9 - This verse supports the message of Chapter 39.

Chapter 37 explores the theme of 'Wrestling with Doubt'. In this chapter, we reflect on how God's presence, grace, and calling are evident in our lives despite our imperfections. This devotional draws from scripture to provide comfort, guidance, and inspiration as you grow in faith.

Journal Prompt: What truth stood out to you in Chapter 37? How can you live this out today?

Quote: "You are still chosen, even in your wrestling with doubt season."

Prayer: Lord, help me embrace Your purpose for me, especially in this area of wrestling with doubt.

Chapter 38: Wrestling with Doubt - Lesson 38

Scripture: Titus 3:5 - This verse supports the message of Chapter 40.

Chapter 38 explores the theme of 'Wrestling with Doubt'. In this chapter, we reflect on how God's presence, grace, and calling are evident in our lives despite our imperfections. This devotional draws from scripture to provide comfort, guidance, and inspiration as you grow in faith.

Journal Prompt: What truth stood out to you in Chapter 38? How can you live this out today?

Quote: "You are still chosen, even in your wrestling with doubt season."

Prayer: Lord, help me embrace Your purpose for me, especially in this area of wrestling with doubt.

Chapter 39: God's Grace & Redemption - Lesson 39

Scripture: Isaiah 1:18 - This verse supports the message of Chapter 41.

Chapter 39 explores the theme of 'God's Grace & Redemption'. In this chapter, we reflect on how God's presence, grace, and calling are evident in our lives despite our imperfections. This devotional draws from scripture to provide comfort, guidance, and inspiration as you grow in faith.

Journal Prompt: What truth stood out to you in Chapter 39? How can you live this out today?

Quote: "You are still chosen, even in your god's grace & redemption season."

Prayer: Lord, help me embrace Your purpose for me, especially in this area of god's grace & redemption.

Chapter 40: God's Grace & Redemption - Lesson 40

Scripture: Romans 6:14 - This verse supports the message of Chapter 42.

Chapter 40 explores the theme of 'God's Grace & Redemption'. In this chapter, we reflect on how God's presence, grace, and calling are evident in our lives despite our imperfections. This devotional draws from scripture to provide comfort, guidance, and inspiration as you grow in faith.

Journal Prompt: What truth stood out to you in Chapter 40? How can you live this out today?

Quote: "You are still chosen, even in your god's grace & redemption season."

Prayer: Lord, help me embrace Your purpose for me, especially in this area of god's grace & redemption.

Chapter 41: God's Grace & Redemption - Lesson 41

Scripture: 2 Corinthians 5:17 - This verse supports the message of Chapter 43.

Chapter 41 explores the theme of 'God's Grace & Redemption'. In this chapter, we reflect on how God's presence, grace, and calling are evident in our lives despite our imperfections. This devotional draws from scripture to provide comfort, guidance, and inspiration as you grow in faith.

Journal Prompt: What truth stood out to you in Chapter 41? How can you live this out today?

Quote: "You are still chosen, even in your god's grace & redemption season."

Prayer: Lord, help me embrace Your purpose for me, especially in this area of god's grace & redemption.

Chapter 42: God's Grace & Redemption - Lesson 42

Scripture: Lamentations 3:22-23 - This verse supports the message of Chapter 44.

Chapter 42 explores the theme of 'God's Grace & Redemption'. In this chapter, we reflect on how God's presence, grace, and calling are evident in our lives despite our imperfections. This devotional draws from scripture to provide comfort, guidance, and inspiration as you grow in faith.

Journal Prompt: What truth stood out to you in Chapter 42? How can you live this out today?

Quote: "You are still chosen, even in your god's grace & redemption season."

Prayer: Lord, help me embrace Your purpose for me, especially in this area of god's grace & redemption.

Chapter 43: God's Grace & Redemption - Lesson 43

Scripture: John 1:16 - This verse supports the message of Chapter 45.

Chapter 43 explores the theme of 'God's Grace & Redemption'. In this chapter, we reflect on how God's presence, grace, and calling are evident in our lives despite our imperfections. This devotional draws from scripture to provide comfort, guidance, and inspiration as you grow in faith.

Journal Prompt: What truth stood out to you in Chapter 43? How can you live this out today?

Quote: "You are still chosen, even in your god's grace & redemption season."

Prayer: Lord, help me embrace Your purpose for me, especially in this area of god's grace & redemption.

Chapter 44: God's Grace & Redemption - Lesson 44

Scripture: Romans 8:1 - This verse supports the message of Chapter 46.

Chapter 44 explores the theme of 'God's Grace & Redemption'. In this chapter, we reflect on how God's presence, grace, and calling are evident in our lives despite our imperfections. This devotional draws from scripture to provide comfort, guidance, and inspiration as you grow in faith.

Journal Prompt: What truth stood out to you in Chapter 44? How can you live this out today?

Quote: "You are still chosen, even in your god's grace & redemption season."

Prayer: Lord, help me embrace Your purpose for me, especially in this area of god's grace & redemption.

Chapter 45: God's Grace & Redemption - Lesson 45

Scripture: Hebrews 4:16 - This verse supports the message of Chapter 47.

Chapter 45 explores the theme of 'God's Grace & Redemption'. In this chapter, we reflect on how God's presence, grace, and calling are evident in our lives despite our imperfections. This devotional draws from scripture to provide comfort, guidance, and inspiration as you grow in faith.

Journal Prompt: What truth stood out to you in Chapter 45? How can you live this out today?

Quote: "You are still chosen, even in your god's grace & redemption season."

Prayer: Lord, help me embrace Your purpose for me, especially in this area of god's grace & redemption.

Chapter 46: God's Grace & Redemption - Lesson 46

Scripture: Colossians 1:13-14 - This verse supports the message of Chapter 48.

Chapter 46 explores the theme of 'God's Grace & Redemption'. In this chapter, we reflect on how God's presence, grace, and calling are evident in our lives despite our imperfections. This devotional draws from scripture to provide comfort, guidance, and inspiration as you grow in faith.

Journal Prompt: What truth stood out to you in Chapter 46? How can you live this out today?

Quote: "You are still chosen, even in your god's grace & redemption season."

Prayer: Lord, help me embrace Your purpose for me, especially in this area of god's grace & redemption.

Chapter 47: God's Grace & Redemption - Lesson 47

Scripture: Psalm 103:12 - This verse supports the message of Chapter 49.

Chapter 47 explores the theme of 'God's Grace & Redemption'. In this chapter, we reflect on how God's presence, grace, and calling are evident in our lives despite our imperfections. This devotional draws from scripture to provide comfort, guidance, and inspiration as you grow in faith.

Journal Prompt: What truth stood out to you in Chapter 47? How can you live this out today?

Quote: "You are still chosen, even in your god's grace & redemption season."

Prayer: Lord, help me embrace Your purpose for me, especially in this area of god's grace & redemption.

Chapter 48: God's Grace & Redemption - Lesson 48

Scripture: 1 Peter 5:10 - This verse supports the message of Chapter 50.

Chapter 48 explores the theme of 'God's Grace & Redemption'. In this chapter, we reflect on how God's presence, grace, and calling are evident in our lives despite our imperfections. This devotional draws from scripture to provide comfort, guidance, and inspiration as you grow in faith.

Journal Prompt: What truth stood out to you in Chapter 48? How can you live this out today?

Quote: "You are still chosen, even in your god's grace & redemption season."

Prayer: Lord, help me embrace Your purpose for me, especially in this area of god's grace & redemption.

Chapter 49: God's Grace & Redemption - Lesson 49

Scripture: Proverbs 19:21 - This verse supports the message of Chapter 51.

Chapter 49 explores the theme of 'God's Grace & Redemption'. In this chapter, we reflect on how God's presence, grace, and calling are evident in our lives despite our imperfections. This devotional draws from scripture to provide comfort, guidance, and inspiration as you grow in faith.

Journal Prompt: What truth stood out to you in Chapter 49? How can you live this out today?

Quote: "You are still chosen, even in your god's grace & redemption season."

Prayer: Lord, help me embrace Your purpose for me, especially in this area of god's grace & redemption.

Chapter 50: God's Grace & Redemption - Lesson 50

Scripture: Jeremiah 29:11 - This verse supports the message of Chapter 52.

Chapter 50 explores the theme of 'God's Grace & Redemption'. In this chapter, we reflect on how God's presence, grace, and calling are evident in our lives despite our imperfections. This devotional draws from scripture to provide comfort, guidance, and inspiration as you grow in faith.

Journal Prompt: What truth stood out to you in Chapter 50? How can you live this out today?

Quote: "You are still chosen, even in your god's grace & redemption season."

Prayer: Lord, help me embrace Your purpose for me, especially in this area of god's grace & redemption.

Chapter 51: Walking in Purpose - Lesson 51

Scripture: Psalm 37:23 - This verse supports the message of Chapter 53.

Chapter 51 explores the theme of 'Walking in Purpose'. In this chapter, we reflect on how God's presence, grace, and calling are evident in our lives despite our imperfections. This devotional draws from scripture to provide comfort, guidance, and inspiration as you grow in faith.

Journal Prompt: What truth stood out to you in Chapter 51? How can you live this out today?

Quote: "You are still chosen, even in your walking in purpose season."

Prayer: Lord, help me embrace Your purpose for me, especially in this area of walking in purpose.

Chapter 52: Walking in Purpose - Lesson 52

Scripture: Ephesians 4:1 - This verse supports the message of Chapter 54.

Chapter 52 explores the theme of 'Walking in Purpose'. In this chapter, we reflect on how God's presence, grace, and calling are evident in our lives despite our imperfections. This devotional draws from scripture to provide comfort, guidance, and inspiration as you grow in faith.

Journal Prompt: What truth stood out to you in Chapter 52? How can you live this out today?

Quote: "You are still chosen, even in your walking in purpose season."

Prayer: Lord, help me embrace Your purpose for me, especially in this area of walking in purpose.

Chapter 53: Walking in Purpose - Lesson 53

Scripture: John 10:10 - This verse supports the message of Chapter 55.

Chapter 53 explores the theme of 'Walking in Purpose'. In this chapter, we reflect on how God's presence, grace, and calling are evident in our lives despite our imperfections. This devotional draws from scripture to provide comfort, guidance, and inspiration as you grow in faith.

Journal Prompt: What truth stood out to you in Chapter 53? How can you live this out today?

Quote: "You are still chosen, even in your walking in purpose season."

Prayer: Lord, help me embrace Your purpose for me, especially in this area of walking in purpose.

Chapter 54: Walking in Purpose - Lesson 54

Scripture: Philippians 1:6 - This verse supports the message of Chapter 56.

Chapter 54 explores the theme of 'Walking in Purpose'. In this chapter, we reflect on how God's presence, grace, and calling are evident in our lives despite our imperfections. This devotional draws from scripture to provide comfort, guidance, and inspiration as you grow in faith.

Journal Prompt: What truth stood out to you in Chapter 54? How can you live this out today?

Quote: "You are still chosen, even in your walking in purpose season."

Prayer: Lord, help me embrace Your purpose for me, especially in this area of walking in purpose.

Chapter 55: Walking in Purpose - Lesson 55

Scripture: Isaiah 30:21 - This verse supports the message of Chapter 57.

Chapter 55 explores the theme of 'Walking in Purpose'. In this chapter, we reflect on how God's presence, grace, and calling are evident in our lives despite our imperfections. This devotional draws from scripture to provide comfort, guidance, and inspiration as you grow in faith.

Journal Prompt: What truth stood out to you in Chapter 55? How can you live this out today?

Quote: "You are still chosen, even in your walking in purpose season."

Prayer: Lord, help me embrace Your purpose for me, especially in this area of walking in purpose.

Chapter 56: Walking in Purpose - Lesson 56

Scripture: Romans 12:2 - This verse supports the message of Chapter 58.

Chapter 56 explores the theme of 'Walking in Purpose'. In this chapter, we reflect on how God's presence, grace, and calling are evident in our lives despite our imperfections. This devotional draws from scripture to provide comfort, guidance, and inspiration as you grow in faith.

Journal Prompt: What truth stood out to you in Chapter 56? How can you live this out today?

Quote: "You are still chosen, even in your walking in purpose season."

Prayer: Lord, help me embrace Your purpose for me, especially in this area of walking in purpose.

Chapter 57: Walking in Purpose - Lesson 57

Scripture: Ecclesiastes 3:1 - This verse supports the message of Chapter 59.

Chapter 57 explores the theme of 'Walking in Purpose'. In this chapter, we reflect on how God's presence, grace, and calling are evident in our lives despite our imperfections. This devotional draws from scripture to provide comfort, guidance, and inspiration as you grow in faith.

Journal Prompt: What truth stood out to you in Chapter 57? How can you live this out today?

Quote: "You are still chosen, even in your walking in purpose season."

Prayer: Lord, help me embrace Your purpose for me, especially in this area of walking in purpose.

Chapter 58: Walking in Purpose - Lesson 58

Scripture: Colossians 3:23 - This verse supports the message of Chapter 60.

Chapter 58 explores the theme of 'Walking in Purpose'. In this chapter, we reflect on how God's presence, grace, and calling are evident in our lives despite our imperfections. This devotional draws from scripture to provide comfort, guidance, and inspiration as you grow in faith.

Journal Prompt: What truth stood out to you in Chapter 58? How can you live this out today?

Quote: "You are still chosen, even in your walking in purpose season."

Prayer: Lord, help me embrace Your purpose for me, especially in this area of walking in purpose.

Chapter 59: Walking in Purpose - Lesson 59

Scripture: Matthew 5:16 - This verse supports the message of Chapter 61.

Chapter 59 explores the theme of 'Walking in Purpose'. In this chapter, we reflect on how God's presence, grace, and calling are evident in our lives despite our imperfections. This devotional draws from scripture to provide comfort, guidance, and inspiration as you grow in faith.

Journal Prompt: What truth stood out to you in Chapter 59? How can you live this out today?

Quote: "You are still chosen, even in your walking in purpose season."

Prayer: Lord, help me embrace Your purpose for me, especially in this area of walking in purpose.

Chapter 60: Walking in Purpose - Lesson 60

Scripture: Galatians 6:9 - This verse supports the message of Chapter 62.

Chapter 60 explores the theme of 'Walking in Purpose'. In this chapter, we reflect on how God's presence, grace, and calling are evident in our lives despite our imperfections. This devotional draws from scripture to provide comfort, guidance, and inspiration as you grow in faith.

Journal Prompt: What truth stood out to you in Chapter 60? How can you live this out today?

Quote: "You are still chosen, even in your walking in purpose season."

Prayer: Lord, help me embrace Your purpose for me, especially in this area of walking in purpose.

Chapter 61: Walking in Purpose - Lesson 61

Scripture: Matthew 6:33 - This verse supports the message of Chapter 63.

Chapter 61 explores the theme of 'Walking in Purpose'. In this chapter, we reflect on how God's presence, grace, and calling are evident in our lives despite our imperfections. This devotional draws from scripture to provide comfort, guidance, and inspiration as you grow in faith.

Journal Prompt: What truth stood out to you in Chapter 61? How can you live this out today?

Quote: "You are still chosen, even in your walking in purpose season."

Prayer: Lord, help me embrace Your purpose for me, especially in this area of walking in purpose.

Chapter 62: Walking in Purpose - Lesson 62

Scripture: Luke 9:23 - This verse supports the message of Chapter 64.

Chapter 62 explores the theme of 'Walking in Purpose'. In this chapter, we reflect on how God's presence, grace, and calling are evident in our lives despite our imperfections. This devotional draws from scripture to provide comfort, guidance, and inspiration as you grow in faith.

Journal Prompt: What truth stood out to you in Chapter 62? How can you live this out today?

Quote: "You are still chosen, even in your walking in purpose season."

Prayer: Lord, help me embrace Your purpose for me, especially in this area of walking in purpose.

Chapter 63: Living Chosen Daily - Lesson 63

Scripture: Psalm 34:1 - This verse supports the message of Chapter 65.

Chapter 63 explores the theme of 'Living Chosen Daily'. In this chapter, we reflect on how God's presence, grace, and calling are evident in our lives despite our imperfections. This devotional draws from scripture to provide comfort, guidance, and inspiration as you grow in faith.

Journal Prompt: What truth stood out to you in Chapter 63? How can you live this out today?

Quote: "You are still chosen, even in your living chosen daily season."

Prayer: Lord, help me embrace Your purpose for me, especially in this area of living chosen daily.

Chapter 64: Living Chosen Daily - Lesson 64

Scripture: Romans 12:1 - This verse supports the message of Chapter 66.

Chapter 64 explores the theme of 'Living Chosen Daily'. In this chapter, we reflect on how God's presence, grace, and calling are evident in our lives despite our imperfections. This devotional draws from scripture to provide comfort, guidance, and inspiration as you grow in faith.

Journal Prompt: What truth stood out to you in Chapter 64? How can you live this out today?

Quote: "You are still chosen, even in your living chosen daily season."

Prayer: Lord, help me embrace Your purpose for me, especially in this area of living chosen daily.

Chapter 65: Living Chosen Daily - Lesson 65

Scripture: Philippians 4:13 - This verse supports the message of Chapter 67.

Chapter 65 explores the theme of 'Living Chosen Daily'. In this chapter, we reflect on how God's presence, grace, and calling are evident in our lives despite our imperfections. This devotional draws from scripture to provide comfort, guidance, and inspiration as you grow in faith.

Journal Prompt: What truth stood out to you in Chapter 65? How can you live this out today?

Quote: "You are still chosen, even in your living chosen daily season."

Prayer: Lord, help me embrace Your purpose for me, especially in this area of living chosen daily.

Chapter 66: Living Chosen Daily - Lesson 66

Scripture: Colossians 2:6-7 - This verse supports the message of Chapter 68.

Chapter 66 explores the theme of 'Living Chosen Daily'. In this chapter, we reflect on how God's presence, grace, and calling are evident in our lives despite our imperfections. This devotional draws from scripture to provide comfort, guidance, and inspiration as you grow in faith.

Journal Prompt: What truth stood out to you in Chapter 66? How can you live this out today?

Quote: "You are still chosen, even in your living chosen daily season."

Prayer: Lord, help me embrace Your purpose for me, especially in this area of living chosen daily.

Chapter 67: Living Chosen Daily - Lesson 67

Scripture: 2 Peter 1:10 - This verse supports the message of Chapter 69.

Chapter 67 explores the theme of 'Living Chosen Daily'. In this chapter, we reflect on how God's presence, grace, and calling are evident in our lives despite our imperfections. This devotional draws from scripture to provide comfort, guidance, and inspiration as you grow in faith.

Journal Prompt: What truth stood out to you in Chapter 67? How can you live this out today?

Quote: "You are still chosen, even in your living chosen daily season."

Prayer: Lord, help me embrace Your purpose for me, especially in this area of living chosen daily.

Chapter 68: Living Chosen Daily - Lesson 68

Scripture: 1 Thessalonians 5:16-18 - This verse supports the message of Chapter 70.

Chapter 68 explores the theme of 'Living Chosen Daily'. In this chapter, we reflect on how God's presence, grace, and calling are evident in our lives despite our imperfections. This devotional draws from scripture to provide comfort, guidance, and inspiration as you grow in faith.

Journal Prompt: What truth stood out to you in Chapter 68? How can you live this out today?

Quote: "You are still chosen, even in your living chosen daily season."

Prayer: Lord, help me embrace Your purpose for me, especially in this area of living chosen daily.

Chapter 69: Living Chosen Daily - Lesson 69

Scripture: John 15:5 - This verse supports the message of Chapter 71.

Chapter 69 explores the theme of 'Living Chosen Daily'. In this chapter, we reflect on how God's presence, grace, and calling are evident in our lives despite our imperfections. This devotional draws from scripture to provide comfort, guidance, and inspiration as you grow in faith.

Journal Prompt: What truth stood out to you in Chapter 69? How can you live this out today?

Quote: "You are still chosen, even in your living chosen daily season."

Prayer: Lord, help me embrace Your purpose for me, especially in this area of living chosen daily.

Chapter 70: Living Chosen Daily - Lesson 70

Scripture: Galatians 2:20 - This verse supports the message of Chapter 72.

Chapter 70 explores the theme of 'Living Chosen Daily'. In this chapter, we reflect on how God's presence, grace, and calling are evident in our lives despite our imperfections. This devotional draws from scripture to provide comfort, guidance, and inspiration as you grow in faith.

Journal Prompt: What truth stood out to you in Chapter 70? How can you live this out today?

Quote: "You are still chosen, even in your living chosen daily season."

Prayer: Lord, help me embrace Your purpose for me, especially in this area of living chosen daily.

Made in United States
Orlando, FL
21 June 2025